STARTING SCIENCE

ELECTRICITY AND MAGNETISM

KAY DAVIES
AND
WENDY OLDFIELD

STECK-VAUGHN
LIBRARY
A Division of Steck-Vaughn Company

Austin, Texas

Starting Science

Books in the series

About This Book

Electricity and Magnetism introduces children to these forces and how we harness them for our use. Special attention is given to the dangers of using electricity and investigations with electricity are always restricted to using batteries. The children learn how to make a circuit and further activities are based on this simple procedure. The invisible power of magnetism is investigated and also how electricity can be used to make a magnet.

This book provides an introduction to methods in scientific inquiry and recording. The activities and investigations are designed to be straightforward but fun, and flexible according to the abilities of the children.

The main picture and its commentary may be taken as an introduction to the topic or as a focal point for further discussion. Each chapter can form a basis for extended topic work.

Teachers and parents will find that in using this book, they are reinforcing the other core subjects of language and mathematics. Through its topical approach **Electricity and Magnetism** covers aspects of the following subjects: exploration of science, types and uses of materials, earth and atmosphere, forces, electricity and magnetism, energy, and using light and electromagnetic radiation.

©Copyright this edition 1992
Steck-Vaughn Company

Editors: Cally Chambers, Susan Wilson

Typeset by Multifacit Graphics, Keyport, NJ
Printed in Italy by Rotolito Lombarda S.p.A., Milan
Bound in the U.S. by Lake Book, Melrose Park, IL
1 2 3 4 5 6 7 8 9 0 LB 96 95 94 93 92

Library of Congress Cataloging-in-Publication Data

Davies, Kay.
    Electricity and magnetism / written by Kay Davies and Wendy Oldfield.
        p.   cm. — (Starting science)
    Includes bibliographical references (p. 31) and index.
    Summary: Text, illustrations, and suggested activities introduce the forces of electricity and magnetism and how they work.
    ISBN 0-8114-3004-9
    1. Electricity — Juvenile literature. 2. Electricity — Experiments — Juvenile literature. 3. Electric circuits — Juvenile literature. 4. Magnetism — Juvenile literature. 5. Magnetism — Experiments — Juvenile literature [1. Electricity — Experiments. 2. Magnetism — Experiments. 3. Experiments.] I. Oldfield, Wendy. II. Title. III. Series: Davies, Kay. Starting science.
QC527.2.D38 1992   91-30069
537—dc20   CIP AC

CONTENTS

The words that first appear in **bold** in the text or captions are explained in the glossary.

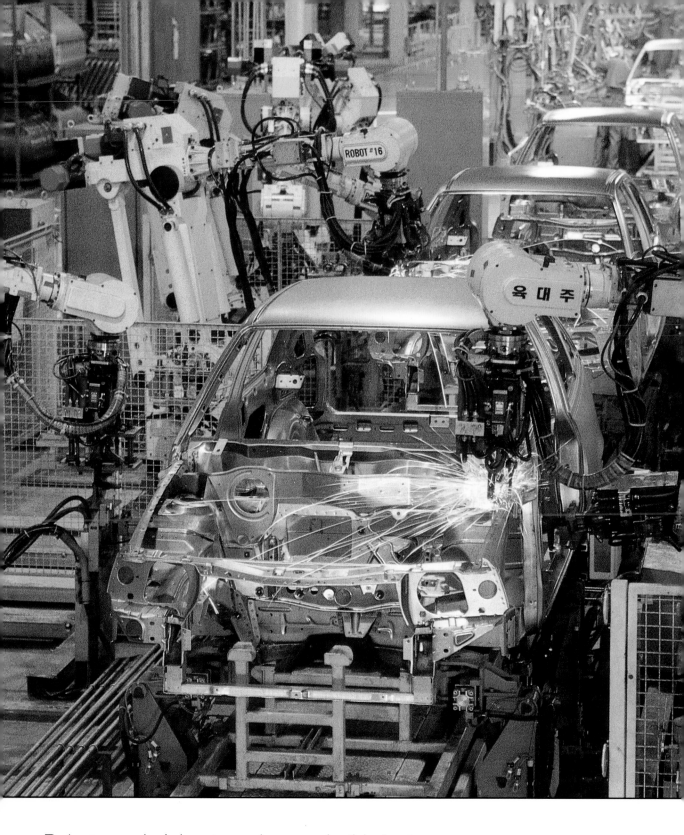

Robots are helping to make cars in this factory.
Electricity provides the **power** that moves the robots.

DRIVING FORCE

What is something powerful that you cannot see?
Electricity.

Electricity is generated, or made, in power stations.
It flows as an electric **current** along wires into buildings.

We use electricity in our homes, at school, and at work.
It can make light, heat, sound, and movement.

How many electrical things can you find in this room?

Make a chart to show if the electricity makes light, heat,
sound, or movement. It may do more than one.

Electrical item	Light	Heat	Sound	Movement
T.V.				
Iron				

Large **cables** carry electricity from power stations to our towns.
The cables are high above the ground, safely out of reach.

DANGER — DON'T TOUCH!

Most homes have much electric equipment.
Every machine has a **plug**, a cord, and a switch.

The plug connects the machine to the electric
power supply. Electric current flows through
the cord to the switch.

Electric current can be dangerous. Never play with plugs,
cords, switches, or **sockets**. You could get a painful
electric shock. You could even get killed.

In the first picture there are five things wrong with the
way electricity is being used. What are they?

The second picture shows you how it should be used.

BATTERY-DRIVEN

Some electric machines do not have plugs and cords. They get electric power from **batteries**.

Batteries make electricity when and where it is needed. We can take them with us wherever we go.

A battery can be as small as your thumbnail or bigger than a shoe box.

Batteries are safe to use, but they don't last forever.

When the power is used up they have to be replaced or **recharged**.

These all use batteries. Can you think of any more?

Electricity makes the toy robot move.
The electric power is made in a battery inside it.

These race cars are like an electric current. The race track is their **circuit**. They must go all around their circuit.

RETURN TO SENDER

Electricity must have a complete pathway to travel around. We call this pathway a circuit.

MAKE A LIGHT CIRCUIT

Get a battery, a light bulb in a holder, and two plastic-coated wires with alligator clips at each end.

Clip one end of each wire to the battery.
Clip the other end of each wire to the bulb holder.

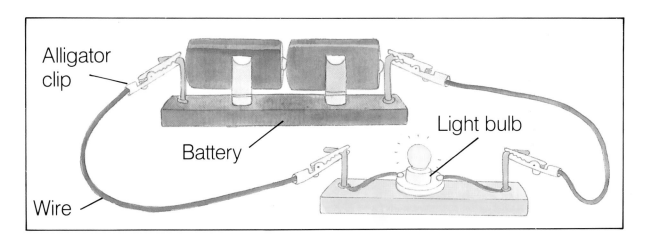

The electric current flows from the battery along the wire. It passes through the bulb and lights it.

The electricity flows back to the battery along the other wire.

If part of the circuit is not connected, the electricity will not flow at all. Unclip one wire to see for yourself.

The children are having fun on the carnival ride.
Switches make the lights flash on and off.

MAKE AND BREAK

When we use an electric appliance, we need a switch to turn it on or off.
When we switch it on, we complete the electric circuit. Electricity flows around.
When we switch it off, the circuit is broken. The electricity stops flowing around.

USE A SWITCH IN A CIRCUIT

Make a room out of a shoe box. Cut holes for windows and doors. Make a hole in the ceiling for a bulb to fit in.

Clip two plastic-coated wires to the bulb holder. Rest the holder on the roof with the light inside. Finish the circuit with a battery, a switch, and one more wire.

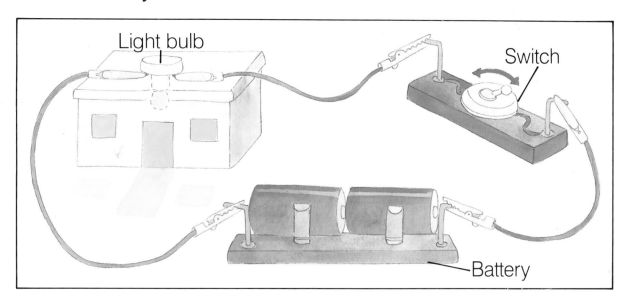

Turn the light on and off with your switch.

PASSING THROUGH

Electricity can flow through some materials. But it cannot flow through others.

Materials that carry electricity are called **conductors**. Wires are made of metal. Metal is a good conductor.

TESTING CONDUCTORS

Collect things made from different materials like metal, wood, cardboard, and plastic. Set up a circuit like this.

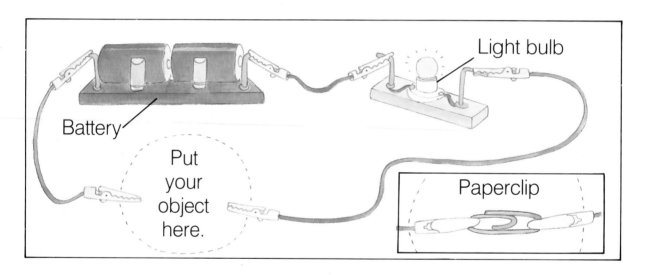

Touch the alligator clips together to test your bulb.

Then, one at a time, put each object into your circuit, by fastening an alligator clip to each end of it.

Some objects conduct electricity to complete the circuit and light the bulb. Which ones do? Which ones don't?

The train speeds through the countryside.
Electricity from the wires above makes it move.

It is very dangerous if wires touch when the **insulator** is
taken away. Never play with wires or cables.

SHORT CIRCUIT

An electric cord is made up of wires covered by an insulator. An insulator is something that does not conduct electricity. It keeps the wires from touching each other.

TESTING AN INSULATOR

Make a "Who lives where" card out of cardboard. Cut three long, thin strips of aluminum foil.

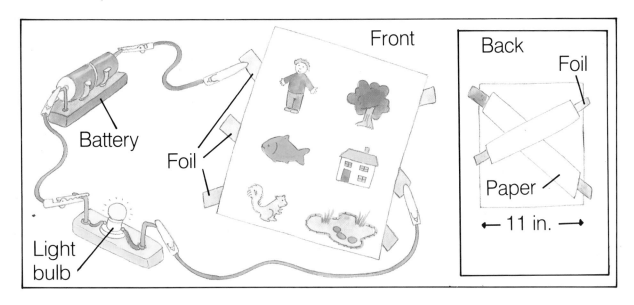

Stick one piece of foil on the back from the squirrel to its tree. Leave some foil sticking out on each side.

Cover the foil with paper for insulation. Match up the other pictures with foil and insulate them too.

Put the card in a circuit. Then test it. When you match the pictures correctly, the light will come on.

SHOCKING EXPERIENCE

Lightning is caused by **static electricity**.

Static electricity can build up when certain things rub against each other.

The electricity passes between two objects and makes a flash.

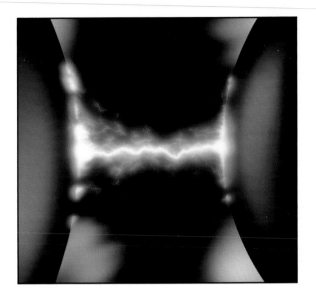

Rub a balloon on your sleeve. Will the balloon stick to the wall?

Comb your hair with a plastic comb. What happens to your hair?

Put the comb near some paper scraps. What happens to them?

Collect things made out of plastic, wood, and metal.

Rub them with a wool cloth. Which ones can pick up scraps of paper? They hold static elecricity.

A flash of lightning from the clouds lights up the sky.
It has the power to damage buildings and trees.

MAGNET MAGIC

Magnets are made of metal, usually iron. A bar magnet is straight. Others can be shaped like a horseshoe.

Magnets pull some materials toward them. This is called attraction.

Collect objects made of different things.

Which ones are attracted by a magnet? What are they made of?

Make a chart showing which objects were attracted to the magnet.

What happens when you put the ends of two bar magnets together?

Turn them the other way around. Does the same thing happen?

Now turn only one around. What happens this time?

Can you feel anything when you hold the magnets together?

Travel games are fun to play with. Tiny magnets inside the pieces hold them to the boards, as if by magic.

STRONG ATTRACTION

The Earth is like a giant magnet. It pulls the needle in a **compass** to point along a north — south line. This happens because the needle in a compass is also a magnet.

You can make your own needle into a magnet.

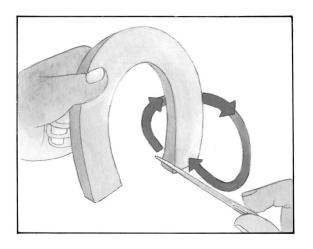

Gently stroke a needle many times with one end of a magnet.

Always move the magnet the same way from one end of the needle to the other.

The needle is now a magnet. It can attract a pin.

Tie a piece of thread to the middle of the needle. Tie the other end to a pencil.

Hang the needle inside a jar like this.

When it stops swinging it will point north — south.

Test this with a compass.

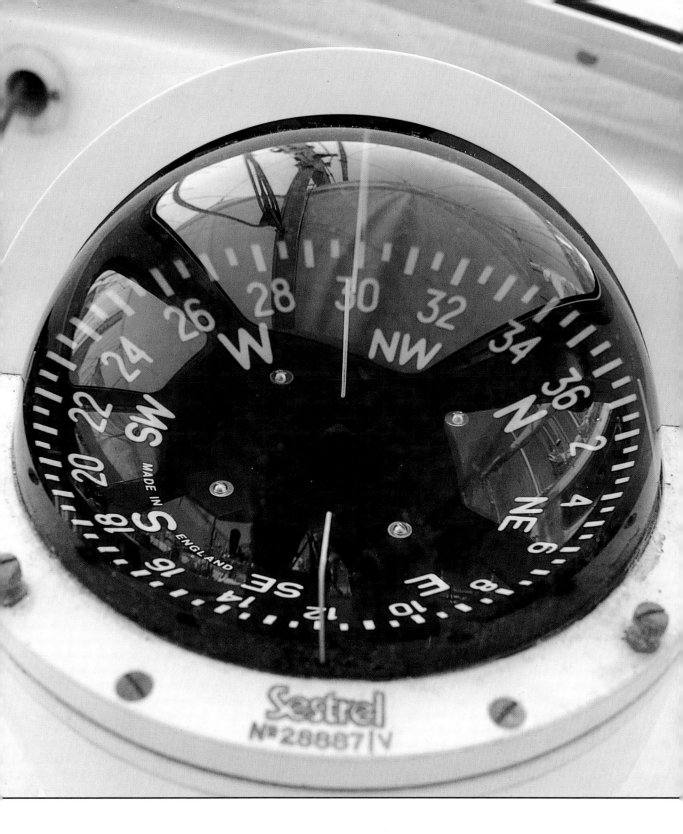

The ship's compass is magnetic. It always points north.
It helps the sailors find their way.

The attraction works even through paper. Magnets inside the objects hold pictures on the refrigerator.

POWERFUL PULL

A magnet can attract metal that is covered by paper. The magnet's force goes through the paper. What else will it go through?

Make a butterfly out of cardboard and decorate it.

Attach a large metal paper clip to the body.

Fold the wings along the broken lines.

Put your butterfly on wood, glass, plastic, paper, and a metal lid.

Move a magnet around underneath.

Can you make your butterfly move each time?

Try another magnet game with a paper clip. Tie a piece of thread to a paper clip. Hold the end of the thread.

Can you make your paper clip rise into the air?
Use your magnet, but don't let it touch the paper clip.

FORCE FIELDS

Magnets are surrounded by invisible force fields. The force fields are strongest at the magnets' **poles**, or ends.

Cover a magnet with a piece of paper.

Sprinkle iron filings over it. Tap the paper gently.

The iron filings show you the shape of the magnetic field.

They show you where the field is strongest, too.

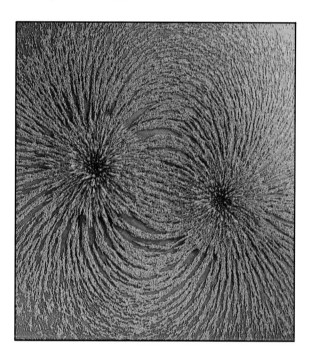

Find lots of magnets to test their strengths.

Try to pick up a string of pins or paper clips with each magnet.

How many will the ends of each magnet hold?

The horseshoe magnet's force pulls the iron filings towards it.
They make a pattern on the clear plastic.

CURRENT ATTRACTION

Electromagnets are special magnets. They can be turned on and off. When an electric current flows around them, they act like magnets. When the current is switched off, the magnet turns off.

USE ELECTRICITY TO MAKE A **MAGNETIC FIELD**

Make this circuit and put a compass on the table. Watch the compass when you bring a magnet near it.

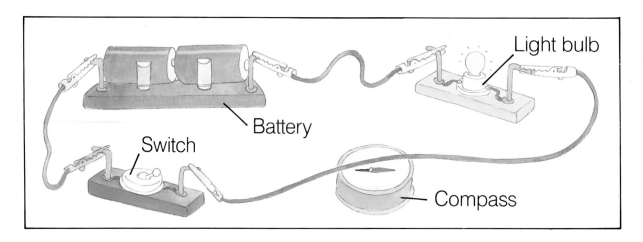

Now hold one of the wires over the compass. Switch the electricity on. Watch what happens to the needle.

Switch it off and turn the battery around. Try the test again. What happens to the needle this time?

When the electricity flows it makes a magnetic field. The magnetic field makes the compass needle move.

When the current is turned on, the electromagnet picks up iron.
When the current goes off, it drops its load.

GLOSSARY

Battery A source of electric current.

Cables Large bundles of wires usually covered with plastic insulation.

Circuit The path followed by an electric current. It must be complete for electricity to flow around it.

Compass A magnetic needle in a case. The needle swings to point along a north — south line.

Conductor A material through which electricity can flow.

Current The flow of electricity.

Insulator A material through which electricity cannot flow.

Magnetic field The area of attraction around a magnet.

Plug The part of an electric cord that fits into an electrical socket.

Poles The ends of a magnet where the force is strongest. There are north and south poles.

Power The energy to make things do something.

Recharge To restore a battery.

Sockets Electric power outlets with openings in which to fit electric plugs or bulbs.

Static electricity An electrical charge that builds up on something; can be caused by rubbing.

FINDING OUT MORE

Books to read:

Electricity by Mark W. Bailey (Raintree Pubs., 1988)
Electricity by Keith Brandt (Troll Assocs., 1985)
Electricity and Magnetism by Terry Jennings, "The Young Scientist Investigates" series (Childrens Press)
Electricity and Magnetism by Gregory Vogt (Franklin Watts, 1986)
Electricity and Magnetism by Kathryn Whyman (Franklin Watts, 1986)
Electricity Turns the World On! by Tom Johnston (Gareth Stevens, 1987)
Experiments with Electricity by Helen Challand, "New True Books" series (Childrens Press, 1986)
Experiments with Magnets by Helen Challand, "New True Books" series (Childrens Press, 1986)
More Power to You by Vickie Cobb (Little, Brown & Co., 1986)
Things at Home by E. Humberstone (EDC Pubs., 1981)

PICTURE ACKNOWLEDGMENTS

Aerofilms Ltd 10; Paul Brierly 26 top; Eye Ubiquitous 8, 12, 21, 24; Chris Fairclough Colour Library 21; J Allan Cash Ltd. 9, 23; © James Minor cover; Science Photo Library 18 top; Wayland Picture Library (Zul Mukhida) 18 bottom, 20, 22, 25, 26 bottom; ZEFA 4, 6, 15, 16, 19, 29
Artwork illustrations by Rebecca Archer. Cover design by Angela Hicks.

INDEX

First published in 1990 by Wayland
(Publishers) Ltd.
©Copyright 1990 Wayland (Publishers) Ltd.